FROM THE ENCHANTED TALES OF

THE BROTHERS GRIMM

BEAUTY AND THE BEAST

First published in Great Britain by Beehive Books, an imprint of
Orbis Publishing Limited, London, 1986.

The Enchanted Tales of Grimm and Andersen are produced by Mushroom Writers' and Artists' Workshop Limited, 9 Newburgh Street, London, W1V 1LH.

Printed in Belgium by Proost
Origination by Newsele SRL (UK)
Typeset by Chambers Wallace of Drury Lane in Monophoto Baskerville

ISBN 0 85613 943 2

FROM THE ENCHANTED TALES OF

THE BROTHERS GRIMM

BEAUTY AND THE BEAST

BEEHIVE BOOKS · LONDON

One day your father hears that a great-great uncle, a sea captain, has died. He has left your father all his possessions: a leaky old ship and a map. Your father believes that the map will lead him to a treasure island. He announces that he is going to hire a crew and set sail in search of the island. Your mother believes that the island is nothing but a fairy story and that your great-great Uncle Pegleg was no better than a pirate. But she goes with her husband anyway.

'You must be good,' she tells you. 'And do as your sisters tell you. If we find the island, I'll bring you back some treasure.'

You stay with your big sister and your bullying bigger sister, your loud, lazy younger brother and your stupid bigger brother. It isn't too bad. Most of the time you keep out of their way. A year passes. The money your parents left begins to run out. You can't pay the servants, so they find other jobs. Then you can't pay the butcher or the milkman. You have to sell the big house and move into a tiny cottage. Your brothers go to work on the farm. Your sisters sit and moan all day for their lost fortune. Everyone but you is convinced that your parents are lost at sea.

If you want to have an adventure and try to make your own fortune without relying on the treasure island, start on page 1.

'That's it,' announces your eldest sister. 'The housemaid has resigned. She was the last one. Now we haven't got any servants.'

'I'm not surprised,' says your second sister. 'We haven't paid anyone for three months. Who's going to do the housework, then?'

'I can't,' says your eldest sister hastily. 'I'm courting. No one will marry me if my hands are all roughened and coarse from housework.'

'Well I can't,' says your second sister. 'I'm delicate.'

'And we can't,' chorus your brothers. 'We work hard all day on the farm.'

There is a long silence. You realise that everyone is looking at you.

'Good,' says your eldest sister. 'That's settled, then. I'm going upstairs to lie down. Bring me some tea at four o'clock.'

'I'm going out,' says your second sister. 'Have my best dress washed and ironed when I get back.'

If you want to do as your sisters say, go to page 30.
Or, if you hate housework, run away. Go to page 28.

You return home, laden with jewels and gold. When you tell your sisters that you must use the magic ring to go back to the Beast as you promised, they rub their eyes with onions to make themselves cry. They weep and wail, moaning that they will be so sad to lose you. But they are really only sorry to lose the riches. When you give them the gold and jewels and tell them about the Beast's wealth, they decide to take your magic ring and go to the castle to steal some more.

Let your sisters grab the ring and go to page 6.
Or put on the ring yourself before your sisters can snatch it and go to page 10.

The path leads over craggy, grey mountains dotted with hungry-looking goats and sheep who stare at you to see if you would make a good meal.

Overhead great beaked hawks hover, watching Lucky. Snow begins to fall and you can just make out your sisters' cottage. You peer at the small light twinkling in the growing gloom. It looks miles away.

Will you carry on until you reach home? Then turn to page 18.
Or, if you think that you will be frozen to a snowman if you carry on tonight, take shelter in the forest. Go to page 21.

In the middle of the night the dragon's colour changes. Starting at the tip of its tail, he turns from blue and green to pink and red. When the end of his nose is bright red, he gives a mighty yawn.

'Excuse me,' you say. 'We came in to shelter from the rain. We wondered if we could stay the night.'

'Well, my good creatures,' says the dragon. 'You may sleep here until morning. As a reward for not waking me, and not stealing my treasure, I will give you some for yourselves.'

The dragon falls asleep again. You and Lucky curl up on the treasure hoard. You sleep quite well, but you would gladly have swopped some priceless jewels for a soft pillow.

Next morning you set out, with a bag of gold and jewels.

If you want to go into the forest, go to page 21.
Or, if you want to follow the road, go left. Go to page 7.
Or turn right. Go to page 31.

You slither down the wet and treacherous path, through a gate and into a field. Stumbling along with your head down against the driving rain, you hear strange noises. Things are whispering and scurrying underfoot. Birds are calling in hoarse cackles. This field is an eerie place. You hurry on.

Suddenly you look up – and see a horrible apparition. Under a strange sort of brown umbrella is an ugly, wrinkled, lumpy face. Under the face is a gnarled hand, beckoning you with a crooked finger.

'Come here!' the thing hisses. 'Say that you like me! Please say that you like me!'

Run away, quickly! Go back to the ghastly castle. Go to page 27.
Or, if the castle scares you more than the thing, run past it to page 24.

Your sisters tug the ring from your finger.

'Don't rub it!' you warn. 'Whatever you do, don't rub the ring!'

'Why?' asks your eldest sister. 'Is it magic? Does it bring treasure? You're trying to keep it all to yourself, selfish beast.' She rubs hard, and instantly disappears! So does your second sister, who was hanging on to her, making sure that she didn't miss out on anything.

They must have been transported to the Beast's castle. You could leave them there. The Beast will certainly know how to deal with them. Then you could stay happily at home with your brothers.

Or, if you remember that the Beast was extremely angry when he thought you were stealing his property, and you think he might hurt your sisters, you could try to rescue them. Go to the Beast's castle. Go to page 35.

A few miles down the road, Lucky becomes tired and heads for home. You walk on until you see a little old lady sitting in a tree.

'I am the king's mother,' she announces, 'but I'm under the spell of a wicked witch. Will you help me? I can't walk, I am too tired and too old.'

She is very ugly. She has a huge nose and a great black hat. You are in an awful hurry. You know that your stupid brother will soon be after you.

If you want to help the old lady as she asks, go to page 26.
Or, if you want to ignore her, carry on down the road. Go to page 20.

With a growl, the Beast rolls his eyes, beats on his chest and grabs you by the neck. His heavy paws shake you until your teeth rattle. With a terrible start you wake up. You are in bed and your beastly brother is shaking you furiously, demanding to know why the fires aren't laid, the breakfast cooked, the water heated . . .

You stagger out of bed and begin another long, tiring day, hoping that you won't fall asleep and dream again.

Gingerly, you creep forward to the pile of treasure, taking no notice of Lucky's warning growls. Pocketing a dozen gold coins, you stretch up to grab a gold bar. Suddenly the whole heap starts to slide and the dragon slides down with it! You are petrified. Your feet feel as if they are glued to the floor! In the twinkle of an eye, Lucky turns herself into a mouse. Just as the dragon opens his huge jaws wide enough to gulp you up, he spots the mouse and whimpers. (All dragons are terrified of mice, of course.)

Lucky pushes you out in front of her and you dash down the steps, dropping your booty as you run.

If you want to run into the forest, go to page 21.
Or, if you want to take the left hand road, go to page 24.

You slip the magic ring onto your finger. In a flash, you land with a bump on your bottom in the castle gardens. Following a delicious smell of baking, you go inside and find that the Beast has prepared a wonderful meal of fragrant herb and mushroom stew and new bread, just for you.

Later you go to your magnificent bedroom. Next to your soft, luxurious feather bed, you find dainty cakes and a huge box of sweets.

Days pass and you grow very fond of the Beast, even though he is so ugly. Then he asks if you will stay with him forever.

Agree, and tell the Beast that you like him very much. Go to page 17.
Or say that you want to go home. Go to page 8.

Promising to return promptly, you take the Beast's ring. The instant you slip it onto your finger you find yourself at home. Your sisters snatch the bag of treasure before you have a chance to hand it over. Then they try to grab your ring. You hang on to it, and accidentally rub it. Instantly the Beast appears. Your sisters cringe away in terror.

The Beast grabs the bag and takes out two gold coins. He gives one to each sister and says, 'Now leave, and don't come back! If I ever catch you bullying or stealing again, I'll turn you into statues!'

Your sisters are glad to get away. They run through the door and along the road. The Beast vanishes.

If you want to follow the Beast to his castle, and thank him for saving you from your sisters, put on the ring again. Go to page 15.
Or, if you want to stay at home and enjoy your freedom, go to page 12.

Without your nasty sisters, home is peaceful. You get on well with your brothers, even if one of them is stupid. They make their own breakfast, fetch you yours in bed, and they are always bringing you presents: fresh eggs and live chickens for you to look after. But you feel guilty. After all, the Beast did get rid of your nasty sisters, and you did promise to return to him.

Rub the ring and dash back to the lonely, waiting Beast. Go to page 8.
Or walk back to the Beast's castle through the forest, so that you have time to make up an excuse for being late on the way. Go to page 15.

You follow the road over the hill. From here it slopes straight down to the sea. You spot your father's ship among the brightly coloured fleet bobbing up and down in the harbour. You hurry to the quay and find the ship's captain. He welcomes you on board and shows you his cargo: vast piles of gold, lengths of silk, chests of teas and spices and beautiful jewels.

You take a bag of treasure for each of your sisters.

'Your parents want me to sell the rest and send on the money,' explains the captain. 'I expect it's all in their letter.'

If you want to head for home at once, go to page 16.
Or, if you are too tired to go home at once, go to an Inn to read your parents' letter first. Go to page 29.

Deep in the forest, you find the Beast standing in his lovely flower garden, weeping bitterly.

'I will give you anything you wish if only you will be nice to me and stop me being the loneliest Beast in the whole wide world,' he sobs.

'Why are you lonely?' you ask, looking around the magnificent castle and grounds.

'Because I'm the ugliest, horriblest Beast ever and nobody likes me. Nobody will be my friend,' he replies.

If you can tell the Beast that he is not horrible, and that you like him enough to be his best friend, go to page 17.
Or, if you want to say that you don't believe he can grant wishes anyway, because he is only a nasty, ugly old Beast, go to page 25.

As you approach the castle you see the Beast's great hairy body lying on a mossy bank under a spray of roses. Hundreds of petals have fallen, covering him with a multi-coloured blanket. With a cry you rush forward and shake the Beast's shoulder. But nothing happens. The Beast's eyes stay closed and his great big fingers are stiff around the single white rose he clutches.

If you like the Beast, shout into his ear and beg him to wake up. Go to page 17.
Or, if you breathe a sigh of relief and say, 'Thank goodness for that! I never liked him much anyway,' go to page 8.

You climb the hill and wander away from the road into the wood. Nestling under a holly bush you see a small clump of snowdrops, the first spring flowers. You bend to pick them. Lucky hisses, but you take no notice.

You grab the stems – and Lucky lashes out with her claws. Ouch! Lucky never scratches. Why should she claw you now? Is she trying to stop you from picking the flowers?

Go ahead and pick them anyway. Go to page 34.
Or, if you want to heed Lucky's warning, leave the snowdrops alone. Go into the forest. Go to page 21.
Or follow the winding path up the hill to the castle at the top. Go to page 27.

The Beast falls at your feet, writhing. You are afraid that you have done something terrible but then, out of the hairy costume steps a handsome young king.

'Thank you,' he says. 'By saying that you like me, you have saved me from a wicked witch's curse!'

The king becomes your best friend. He gives you a wonderful mansion in the grounds of his castle. Lucky comes to stay with you and you all live happily ever after.

Back at the cottage, they are far more pleased to see the jewels than to see you and they are not interested in your adventures at all. They complain that while you were away there was no one to do the cooking and cleaning. Although you are tired and cold after your long journey, your sisters send you straight into the kitchen.

You don't feel like washing the enormous tower of greasy dishes, so you decide to run away.

Dash out through the kitchen door. Go to page 21.
Or, if you couldn't possibly run away without your cat, Lucky, find her and run through the front door. Go to page 24.

The lane becomes darker and darker and narrower and narrower. Overhanging trees stretch out their branches to trip you up and tug at your clothes and Lucky's fur. She hisses. Black thunderclouds gather overhead and it starts to rain. Soon it's pouring. You feel like turning back and running for home. Then you see a light shining in the distance. You hurry towards it. Soon a great castle with tall towers, black ramparts and turrets rises out of the gloom. At the very top of the tallest tower you can see a light at a tiny window.

If you dare to knock at the front door, go to page 27.
Or, if you are too frightened to go near the castle, run down the road. Go to page 24.
Or try to take a short-cut home. Go to page 5.

You are beginning to feel very hot and sticky, and very tired. You look for a shady spot to take a nap. You are very pleased to find a gigantic toadstool growing by the side of the road. You lie under its wide cap, sheltered from the sun. But you don't notice that the toadstool is melting! The cap softens and runs. Waxen blobs drip onto your face. They set in horrible grey lumps, like blisters. You look awful!

The king's mother arrives. She can walk perfectly well!

'I was testing you,' she says. 'As you weren't kind to me, this is your punishment!' She laughs cruelly and shows you your hideous new face in a mirror.

'You will stay like that,' she says, 'until someone remembers that you have been kind to them in the past. Then you may start your adventure again, and look out for me next time!'

But how long will you have to stay?

You come to a sunny forest clearing. There, in the middle of a huge garden, is a beautiful castle. The door is open. You go inside into a grand hall. You call out, but no one answers. You are tired, so you sit down on one of the plump sofas, to take a rest. You don't mean to fall asleep, but soon you are snoring.

You wake up with a guilty start. By your side is a breakfast tray. You eat and drink, then go back out into the garden. There you find butterflies flocking around rose bushes, though everywhere else in the country it is early Spring.

The roses are beautiful and deliciously scented. You can't resist them. You pluck one. Suddenly a huge, hairy brown beast springs out from behind the bush.

'Caught you!' he growls. 'Stealing my roses, eh? I ought to eat you! However, I'm a reasonable Beast. I'll let you go home – if you promise to return here tomorrow.'

If you agree, take the magic ring the Beast gives you. Tomorrow you must rub it, and you will be transported back to the castle. Go to page 11.
Or, if you're afraid of the Beast, and you don't want to come back, go to page 25.

In the morning you set out on the dangerous journey to the port. Your sisters command you to bring back a bag of jewels for each of them.

'What will you bring back for yourself?' asks your younger brother.

'I want nothing but a snowdrop to show that Spring is on the way,' you reply.

You take Lucky, your little black cat, and set out on your travels. After you have walked for several miles, you come to a fork in the road.

If you want to take the muddy lane to the right, go to page 19.
Or, if you prefer to walk along the clean, dry road to the left, go to page 13.

It is dark when you set out for home and you are very tired. So you are taken by surprise when the bearded sailor and his wicked brigand friends leap out from behind the trees, their teeth and swords flashing. They snatch your bags of jewels and tie you to a tree. You think that all is lost until you suddenly remember the magic word. You shout 'abraCATdabra!' and Lucky jumps up in her fine red swashbuckling boots, swinging her sabre. She lunges at the bandits. They drop the jewels in terror, and run. Lucky unties you, turns back into her normal self and curls up at your feet.

When you wake up after a long sleep you find that you are lost. Will you try to find your way through the forest? Then go to page 21. Or follow the track to page 3.

You follow the brick road for two miles, but there's no sign of the cottage. You begin to wonder if you are lost. You turn to ask Lucky, but she has gone!

You hunt high and low, up trees and down foxes' earths. No sign of any cats. You trudge on alone.

After another mile you meet a little old lady. You ask her the way home. She stares at your face for a long time before she replies, 'I can tell you. But only if you will help me first.' She cackles loudly. 'Don't look so frightened, child,' she says, 'I'm not a hag. I'm the mother of the king.'

If you want to help her, go to page 26.
Or, if you have read fairy stories, and you think she looks like a witch, run away. Try to find the way home by yourself. Go to page 20.

The ugly, hairy Beast is sad. He weeps so much that great rivers of tears run down his chest.

'Only you,' he says, between great sighs and sniffs and puffs. 'Only you can save me. I will die if you don't help me. I will die of loneliness if you do not come back to be my friend.'

You are so amazed and feel so sorry for the Beast that you promise to return. The Beast cheers up and takes a handkerchief out of a pocket in his fur. He dabs at his eyes and offers to give you lots of gold to take home to your brothers and sisters. He gives you a magic ring. If you want to come back to him, all you have to do is rub the ring.

If you want to accept the Beast's gold, go to page 2.
Or, if you want to refuse his generous offer, go to page 8.

The king's mother tells you the story of her son. He has been turned into a monstrous Beast by an evil witch. Only if someone shows him true friendship, and says that they like him, even if he is a Beast, will the spell be broken.

She shows you where the Beast-king lives, and the right road to take if you want to go home. Then she hurries away.

If you want to meet the unhappy Beast, go to page 14.
Or, if you want to forget the Beast and go home, go to page 20.

The castle door opens with a groan. You and Lucky creep inside. You climb the stone stairs round and round and up and up. At the top of the tallest tower you find a huge, round chamber. At the top of the room you find a huge heap of gold, silver and jewels. And on top of the treasure you find a huge dragon! The dragon is curled up tightly with the tip of his tail in his mouth. He seems to be fast asleep. Every time he snores a small red flame pops out of his mouth.

If you want to steal some of the treasure, go to page 9.
Or, if you want to wait and see if the dragon will wake up, sit down quietly. Go to page 4.

Driven away by your sisters' nagging, you pack some bread and cheese in a spotted handkerchief and hide it under your pillow. At the crack of dawn next day you creep downstairs, nearly tripping over your cat.

'Do you want to come too, Lucky?' you ask her. She purrs. Lucky knows that you're the only one who will feed her!

The two of you slip out of the door and set off to seek your fortunes. After walking for many hours you come to a river. Three ferrymen offer to row you across.

If you want to choose the first ferryman, go to page 19.
Or, if you want to choose the second ferryman, go to page 7.
Or, if you want to choose the third ferryman, go to page 13.

After a hearty dinner for you and a bowl of milk for Lucky, you curl up on the four-poster bed to read your letter. But before you get past 'We are having a lovely time . . .' you have fallen asleep.

You are jolted awake by a door creaking. You strain your ears and hear muffled footsteps. You sit up. Suddenly the bed curtains are whipped open. A bearded bandit snaps, 'Your treasure bags or your life!'

You are about to hand the bags over when you suddenly remember the magic word. 'AbraCATdabra!' you yell. There is a blinding flash – and Lucky turns into a mighty swordscat! She springs at the bandit, whirling a sabre. He flees in terror.

You grab Lucky and the bags and dash out of the Inn. Go back the way you came. Go to page 16.
Or, if you think the bandit might ambush you, take a different road, go to page 23.

The work is very hard. Every morning you have to get up at four o'clock to clean the cottage, light the fires and make breakfast for your brothers. You are grateful for somewhere to live and food to eat, but your sisters complain all day long.

One day, a sailor comes to the door. He says that your father's ship, which everyone thought had sunk, has come back! He tells you that it is laden with treasure. Your parents, it seems, have stayed on the treasure island, but they have sent you a letter.

The sailor says that one of you must go to the ship to collect the letter and claim the treasure. Of course your sisters are too lazy to go. And your brothers are too busy on the farm. You have to go.

Set out with Lucky the cat at once. Go to page 13. Or, if you'd rather go tomorrow, go to page 22.

After you have been walking for about an hour Lucky begins to meow plaintively.

'I know you're hungry,' you tell her. 'I want my breakfast, too. We'll see if we can find a farmer who'll sell us some milk.'

At the word 'milk', Lucky pricks her whiskers, lifts her tail and darts off ahead. You follow her round the next corner. Coming towards you is a man leading some cows. Lucky is rubbing herself against his boots, purring loudly.

'You couldn't spare us some milk, could you?' you ask.

'Certainly,' replies the farmer. 'I'll give you all the milk you can drink, if you'll lend me your cat for half an hour.'

If you agree to the farmer's offer, follow him to page 36.
Or, if you don't like the idea of lending Lucky to anyone, run away. Go to page 33.

'AbraCATdabra!' you shout.

A flash! A bang! And a mighty swordscat stands before you. She lunges at the rat with her sabre. It takes one look, drops the sack of grain, and scurries away.

Lucky darts about the barn, running into every nook and cranny where rats might nest, sabre whirling. Soon she has the rats on the run. She shepherds them towards the door, and out, through the farmyard and away.

The grateful farmer gives you both all the milk you can drink. Then he offers you a lift on his haycart to the main road. Continue on your way. Go into the forest on page 21.
Or stay on the road. Go to page 7.

Soon you are hopelessly lost. You trudge across a ploughed field in search of a gate, but eventually decide to climb the hedge. You drop down on the other side, covered in scratches and bruises. You look around. Oh no, another ploughed field! You walk on, but Lucky claws your coat and meows loudly.

'Come on, Lucky,' you say, but she just meows louder, digging in her paws and refusing to budge. She points along the hedge. In the distance you see something dark against the opposite hedge. You run over to it, but it's not a gate, it's a well. Lucky is still meowing. Could this be a wishing well?

You drop in a coin.

If you wish to go home, start again. Go to page 1.
Or, if you wish for an adventure, go to page 7.
Or, if you just wish to get out of the field, go to page 19.

You should have taken notice of Lucky. A leprechaun has made his winter home in the middle of the holly bush. To make sure that no one disturbs his hibernation, he has put a spell on the bush. Anyone who touches it falls asleep! The leprechaun's spell has spread to the flowers growing under the bush. The instant your fingers touch the flowers you fall fast asleep.

Luckily for you Lucky knows what to do. She shakes the leprechaun awake and points to the snowdrops.

'Flowers!' says the leprechaun, between yawns. 'Time I was up.' He lifts the spell, and you wake up.

But your troubles aren't over. You're lost.

Take the winding path up the hill. Go to page 27.
Or, if you think your way doesn't lie uphill, cut across the fields. Go to page 33.

Flanking the stone steps of the castle you find two gold statues. You don't remember those being there before. You inspect them closely. You recognise your elder sister by her mouth, wide open for scolding.

The Beast pads up behind you. 'I caught them stealing my gold,' he tells you. 'So I turned them into statues.'

'No!' you exclaim. 'Turn them back! I know they were unkind and greedy, but they don't deserve to be statues! And I thought you were so kind I *liked* you . . .'

Suddenly the Beast falls to the ground. Great strips of his fur curl up and peel away from – a young king!

'Ooooh, I'm so stiff!' complains a familiar voice from the stairs.

'Where's my mirror?' demands another. 'Oh, drat! I've broken a nail!'

Your sisters are back.

'By saying that you like me, you have broken the spell which made me a Beast!' says the king. 'And I have released your sisters. I hope they'll be grateful and be kinder in future. Now you'd better go home. Your parents are there – and they need help to carry in the chests and chests of treasure they've brought . . .'

The farmer leads you to a barn.

'Some pesky rats have been at my grain,' he tells you. 'They've eaten half my best wheat.'

'Lucky can handle any old rat,' you say. 'But why don't your farmyard cats fight them?'

'They did,' says the farmer. 'The rats ate them!'

Suddenly something dashes out from behind a barrel. It's a rat. An *enormous* giant rat – carrying a sack of grain.

Lucky's fur stands on end. Her whiskers twitch. Her tail stiffens and fluffs out. She spits.

Is she afraid, or does she want to fight?

If you can remember the magic word you said at the Inn, go to page 32.
Or, if you haven't been to an Inn, you won't remember the word. Run away with Lucky to page 19.